From LEBANON TO AFRICA AND *America*

MY ROOTS

NADER CHAABAN

Kendall Hunt
publishing company

Cover image © Shutterstock, Inc.
Interior photos courtesy of the author unless otherwise stated.

Kendall Hunt
publishing company

www.kendallhunt.com
Send all inquiries to:
4050 Westmark Drive
Dubuque, IA 52004-1840

This book is dedicated to my best friend, Eric Raymond Freud,
who passed away unexpectedly on December 30, 2010.
Eric, may you rest in peace. You will always be
in my prayers, and you will never be forgotten.

And my mother and father for raising us the right way,
which wasn't always the easy way.

They are always in my heart.

Contents

Introduction

I am Professor Nader Chaaban. I live the comfortable life of an educated professional with a wonderful family in an interesting community. We are all products of our parents' struggles and ambitions for us, as well as our own experiences. This is my story.

About the Author

Dr. Nader H. Chaaban was born in Kabala, Sierra Leone in Africa, where his parents had emigrated from Lebanon. He attended the local DEC Primary School and Kabala Secondary School (Roman Catholic). After completing his secondary school education, he joined his older siblings in the U.S. to further his education. He received his BA and MA in Communication from George Mason University, Fairfax, Virginia, and his Ph.D. in Mass Communication Research from Howard University, Washington, D.C.

He is a full-time professor of communication at Montgomery College in Rockville, Maryland, where he teaches Introduction to Human Communication, Business and Professional Communication, and Interpersonal Communication. He is also an adjunct faculty member at George Mason University where he teaches communication courses including Foundations of Intercultural Communication and Foundations of Mass Communication. He has written instructor's manuals for two widely used communication textbooks.

When he is not teaching or conducting research he spends his time with his boys reading books, checking their homework, traveling, eating out, and watching educational TV shows.

Currently, he and his wife, Lina, and their children reside in Fairfax, Virginia, U.S.A.

Chapter 1

Our Home Town

My family and I lived in Kabala, which is a town in the northern part of Sierra Leone, in West Africa. It is the largest town of the Koinadugu District. The population of the town is approximately 18,000 and growing almost every year. The town lies about eighty miles northeast of the town of Makeni, which is considered the largest city and the economic center of the north-

ern part of Sierra Leone. The people of Kabala are largely Muslims, and the Islamic culture dominates every aspect of the lives of the people. This is where my father, Abu Faiad, settled when he came to Sierra Leone from Lebanon after World War I. At that time, Lebanon was unsettled economically. On the other hand, Sierra Leone, under a British Protectorate, was more stable and open for development. He found that interactions with indigenous African people of the area were cooperative and friendly. Lebanese businessmen started to open shops in Kabala around 1947, and my father was one of the first Lebanese traders to do so. He opened his shop at the center of the town on 2 Kassim Street, Kabala. He had run other businesses before opening his store.

Map of Sierra Leone.
Courtesy of the Perry-Castaneda Library Map Collection, University of Texas at Austin.

His goal was to have a better life and to start a family. He became a businessman with a general store, and he became well known throughout the town, its neighboring villages, and beyond. It was a very friendly town where everyone knew everybody else, and people were always willing to help one another. Everyone recognized my father. He was of average height. He wore western-style pants and shirts and the traditional Arab white embroidered Kufi cap, which is made from a rigid cotton fabric. On the top of the cap, he would always wear a white scarf. He had big, expressive green eyes.

His favorite color combination was white and black. Almost all of his pants were black and most of his shirts were white. Occasionally, he would wear dark blue pants and light blue shirts. He wore sandals with closed toes, and he never liked wearing socks with his shoes. Whatever kind of shoes or sandal he wore, he always made sure the soles of the shoes were comfortable, not stiff.

Map of Lebanon.
Courtesy of the Perry-Castaneda Library Map Collection, University of Texas at Austin.

Since my father retired when he was about sixty-five years old, my mother, Oum Hanney, as she was called, who was a lot younger than my father, took over the business of running our general merchandise store, and she expanded it tremendously. She was a tall woman with straight jet black hair. She wore a dress that went down to her knees with long sleeves and a head scarf. She always wore sandals that were very comfortable on her feet. Sometimes, she would wear flip flops at home. She always wore a very beautiful smile that quickly revealed her kindness and social abilities. She was soft-spoken, except when she got upset; only then would she raise her voice. She married my father around 1948 and joined him the same year in Sierra Leone. She was very young when she left her parents in Lebanon to join my father. She came from a very big family that had ruled the town of Deirntar for a very long time. When she came to Kabala, she learned the common language spoken by everyone, Creole, as my father had done when he came to Sierra Leone. She mastered it in a very short time. She also learned a few words in some of the other dialects in Sierra Leone. One of the most challenging tasks my mother faced was to raise my three stepbrothers from my dad's previous marriage, especially Ali and Muhammed, and my stepsister, Zainab. My stepbrother, Faiad, was the oldest, and he was more mature than his siblings. When we were growing up, I have to credit my mother for not differentiating between her stepchildren and her own children. In fact, to show that she treated all my father's children equally, she agreed to bring her own sister, Aunty Zahideh, to Sierra Leone to marry my stepbrother, Faiad. She loved him so much that she allowed him to marry her own sister. That showed how much she cared for both of them, and she treated them both with dignity and equality.

Also, together with my father, she helped both of my brothers, Ali and Muhammad, to marry their choice of spouse and my sister, Zainab, to marry a young man named Hussein Ossailay. They were marriages that my father favored, and she made them possible, especially by providing the financial support for all of them.

My mother starting out by selling commodities that people needed the most, including cartridges and gun powder for hunting, clothes, and food items like sugar, salt, rice, onions, potatoes, tomatoes, and much more. In fact, she opened stores in neighboring towns and villages where she made weekly visits. Although my mother was now the main breadwinner, my father was never left out of decision making and problem solving in our household. He was greatly respected, and he was the head of our household. I know some people stereotype Middle Eastern men as being strong and their wives as being submissive, but my parents' situation was quite different. My mother ran both our home and the business. My dad was the one who stayed at home, especially with me, as I was the youngest, when my mother went to conduct her business outside our home.

My parents.

My father's daily routine involved helping my mother in our store, reading Islamic books, Arabic newspapers that he received from Saudi Arabia, and, sometimes, magazines. In the evening, he would often visit friends in neighboring villages, especially a village called Senekedugu. This was a trip that I almost never missed, and I usually took some of my friends from the Jaffar, Antar, Basma, and Mackie families. We would chat about school activities and other topics on our way to Senekedugu and back. Our driver, Amadu, would always let me know if he was taking my father to Senekedugu. He knew how much I loved going there and visiting with my father's friends. Whenever we went there my father's friends would provide us with super fresh fruits and vegetables. Before they brought the vegetables and fruits out, they would ask my father if he needed any fruits and vegetables. My father's usual response was no, but his friends would never accept no for an answer. Since our culture is a high-context culture, the answer to the question did not mean much. In a high-context culture, most of the information is either in the physical context or internalized. It is rarely explicit, as in low-context cultures. My father's friends would provide us with as many different fruits and vegetables as possible. When the fruits and vegetables were given to us, we would wash them and start eating them right away. I really loved the bananas, the lettuce, cucumbers, and mangoes. In fact, we would all just indulge ourselves with the vegetables and fruits. We would bring whatever was left back with us to Kabala. On some occasions, we would visit another friend of my father's just a few minutes away from Senedugu to bathe at a little river. That was fabulous and entertaining. We would all get into the water to swim and splash around and then wash ourselves. That was where I enjoyed the best of what nature can offer. One day, my father decided to take one of his Lebanese friends with us to the river. We took food and drinks with us. On our way back, his friend, Abu Muhammad, told my father that was the best therapy anyone can have. I agreed with him. I really loved it, especially when we all used to gather around the food after bathing. This was the closest to nature anyone could experience.

One day, when I went to tell our driver, Amadu, that my father wanted to go for an evening drive to Senekedugu, he told me to tell my father that he was not feeling well and that he was down emotionally. When I told my father what the driver had said, my father said to go back and ask Amadu what he was suffering from and whether he was really upset. Amadu then told me that his wife left him and was now staying with her parents and he was confused. When my father heard that, he convinced Amadu to take us for his evening drive and promised that he would help him. Later, after talking with Amadu's wife, my father realized that the wife did not want to come back to Amadu. On our way to the village, father discussed some of the problems Amadu had with his current wife and asked him what kind of a wife he was looking for. My father also advised him on how to make sure that, if he got married again, he could best make sure that he and his wife would live a peaceful and loving life. Since my father was a religious man, he quoted many verses from the Holy Quran and the Hadiths (sayings) of the holy Prophet Muhammad as well as other Islamic books. He made sure that the driver understood the value of marriage and the responsibilities of both man and wife within the Islamic religion. My father explained to the driver that people should not leave a marriage just because of difficulties or minor problems. As for his children, he always taught us not to be embarrassed by the pride, riches, and successes of others, but for us to work hard to be responsible citizens like our parents. He really never cared about being very rich. His main goal in life was to live a religious life and to make sure his children were successful in whatever they did.

The new task of finding Amadu a wife was a very easy task for my father, as it turned out. When we got to the first village, Sokurala, my father told one of his friends about his intention of finding our driver a wife. Later, on our way back from Senekedugu, a young lady about the age of 18 was waiting with her parents to see our driver. Arrangements were made for the ceremony, and our driver was a very happy man on our way back home. My father looked at him and said, "Everything is possible in the eyes of God." It was all smiles on the driver's face. He was from the Madingo tribe, and eventually had three children with his new wife. Now he would have a stable life again. This was just one example of how my father helped people, especially those closest to him.

On the days that he did not want to visit his friends in Senekedugu and other neighboring villages, he would take a walk with his friends in Kabala. Among his circle of friends were Hajj Habib, Hajj Mustapha, Hajj Ali, and others. These three were Lebanese businessmen who were also brothers. They would walk slowly for almost an hour around the town of Kabala. Whenever they got tired, they would sit for about half an hour and then continued to walk until dark. Sometimes, they would sit in the nice mall by the Kabala Police Station and Post Office and eat fresh mangoes after washing them. Each one of them would bring a pocket knife to peel the mangoes before eating them. They would sit in a semi-circle and just enjoy the delicious flavor. Sometimes at night my mother would visit her sister, my Aunt Zahideh, (Oum Munir, as she was also called), while my father was visiting his friends. My father would always come home earlier than my mother. He would lie down on the hammock that we had in our backyard until my mother was home safely. On a few occasions, if it was past 10:00 pm, he would send one of us to go tell my mother it was getting late and that it was time for her to come home. He never wanted her to walk home alone, especially after 10:00 pm.

My father loved meat, especially lamb and goat meat. He slaughtered either a lamb or a goat almost every week at the back of our house. He had all his tools to slaughter animals, including poultry. He would purchase the animals from neighboring villages and share the cost of the animal with one of his friends, and when he slaughtered the animal he would give his friend his or her equal share. One of his closest friends, named Fouzieh, would share the cost and the meat almost once a month. She loved goat meat, but not lamb. So, whenever she let him know that she would like to share the meat, my father would make sure he bought a goat, not a lamb. After he slaughtered the animals, Miss Fouzieh would tell him what part of the animal she wanted and he would cut that section for her. Slaughtering these animals was one of my father's favorite things to do. He considered it an art. After sharing the animal, my father would give my mother and our cook, Pa Kamanda, some of the meat to make different kinds of foods, including raw frakeh, which is very similar to sushi, except this was raw meat. I have to say that this was also one of my favorite dishes. We were told many times about how dangerous it was to eat raw meat and how it might give us food-borne diseases, but we never listened. We compromised our health for the taste of the food. My mother had a special way of fixing this particular kind of food. The meat was ground, mixed with cracked wheat and spices, and put on a plate like a pie. Then she would sprinkle some olive oil on it and serve it with pita bread and fresh radishes. Wow, this was a very delicious homemade food! I have to say that my mother just had a special touch with this particular food. Her hand performed miracles when it came to the flavor. In our opinion, no one could make it tastier or better than my mother.

Another food that my mother would make for us with the fresh meat was fried meat with potatoes and onions. My father used to love this food. This particular dish was normally made for

My father in his late 70s.

lunch. The special ingredient used in this dish was the onion. I loved the way my mother or our cook fried the onions. You could taste the richness and flavor of the onion without the strong smell. Sometimes, when this particular dish was made, we would all sit with my father and eat lunch. My family was not big on breakfast. I believe that is how I got used to not eating breakfast. Breakfast was not one of our favorite meals. Many of us at our house skipped breakfast. We all would start eating during lunch time.

Chapter 2

The Weekly Trip to Bafodia

It was approximately 7:00 am when our driver, Amadu, and his helper, Sieh, started to load the Land Rover to get ready for my mother's Sunday trip to Bafodia. Every Sunday, my mother took this eight-hour round trip to sell goods to shopkeepers in different villages and towns on her way to Bafodia, which is a town approximately thirty-two miles from our home in Kabala. This trip allowed my mother to maintain her business and thereby earn a living so she could take care of our family. Since my father retired, my mother was the main breadwinner in our family. Around 8:00 am the driver told my mother that he was ready for the trip. My father would always read a Du'ah, which is an Islamic prayer, asking Allah to guide my mother through the whole trip so she could return home safely. I am very confident that my father's prayers were always answered by God since my mother always came back safely.

As soon as my mother left on her Sunday trip, my father would relax in his comfortable chair, drink coffee, read his Islamic books, and, often, take short naps. After performing his noon prayers he would start telling our cook, Pa Kamanda, and the rest of the people who worked for us, to prepare my mother's meal, clean the house, and generally get ready for her safe return. All attention in the house would be focused on my mother's arrival. My dad would be looking out for our Land Rover whenever he heard the sound of any vehicle. As for the kids, we would all wait restlessly for her arrival because she would bring back very delicious big bananas, plantains, oranges, and other fruit and vegetables. As soon as the Land Rover pulled up, I, together with my nephews and a few friends who might happen to be around, would rush to the car to get some fruit.

As soon as my mother entered the house, my father would take out his record keeping book and start asking my mother who, among her customers, had received a new loan and who had repaid her. He would calculate how much money she brought back with her, how many items of the different goods she had sold, and the total amount of all the loans she gave out. He would go back and forth over these items with my mother until he was satisfied with the final numbers. While they were doing this, they would be sipping Lebanese coffee and maybe eating a light meal. My mother never ate a heavy meal upon her return. She would wait until dinner before eating something heavy. I guess this was due to the fact that she normally took food and water with her for her trip. One thing that I remember is that as soon as she came back, she always wanted Lebanese coffee and a bottle of cold water.

My mom's first stop on her way to Bafodia was a small town called Dogolonya. She had a few customers there who would buy goods from her like sugar, salt, cement, bb cartridges, clothes, and cigarettes. She gave out loans to some of the shopkeepers who would, in turn, pay her back and then take more goods for the following week.

Her next stops would be three or four small villages, then finally at Bafodia, where people, including Chief Alimamy Salifu Mansary, would be waiting for her. As chief of the village, he had to approve all public financial interactions that took place in Bafodia, commercial and otherwise. He was well respected, and whenever my mother would encounter difficulties or problems in dealing with some of her customers, he would solve it immediately. He was always by my mother's side. She, in return, would make sure he got what he wanted, including gun powder, cartridges, shoes, clothes, and other commodities that he asked for. Some of the items were given to him as gifts, while others were sold to him at a discounted price. She would always get a very warm reception from the villagers that included handshakes, food, sometimes a gift of small farm animals, and hugs from the women. She would make her rounds from one storekeeper to another, including her favorite shopkeeper, Thairu. She would do this in the hot blazing sun. She did not mind the heat. Thairu was a very quiet and soft spoken man who would always make sure my mother was completely happy before she left. Apart from doing business, he would make sure she got her supply of vegetables, fruit, and other items. He always got reimbursed for all the items my mother asked for and received.

After re-supplying her customers and making sure that they got all they needed and asked for, she would head back home, a trip that normally took approximately four hours on a good day. If it was raining, the trip took longer due to challenging conditions such as muddy roads, flooded bridges, and other road hazards caused by rain. Also, on her way back, there were people waiting to be dropped from one village to another or those heading for Kabala. Since public transportation was limited to and from Bafodia and the neighboring villages, this was a chance people got once a week to travel from one point to another, catching a ride in my mother's Land Rover. If they missed this opportunity, then they would have to wait until the following Sunday. Almost everyone in all the villages and towns leading to Bafodia knew my mother and would wait for her on Sunday of every week to discuss their financial and some- times social problems. She was a very generous person who would readily hand out money to those who asked for it if they were able to convince her that they really needed it. On one occasion, she was confronted by a couple who could not afford to buy uniforms so their chil- dren to go to school. Not only did she give them the money to buy their uniforms, but she also gave them money for school fees including tuition, books, and other expenses. She was the kind of lady who would not say "no" to either strangers or people she knew when they asked for a favor.

One week, when my mother left for her Sunday trip to Bafodia, she did not come back at her normal time which was 3:00 pm. My father and aunt became very restless. We waited until 5:00 pm, and then my father decided to send me to check and see if she'd had car trouble or any other problems. I took my motorcycle to make the three hour trip hoping to see my mother on the way to Bafodia. I rode for about three hours. As soon as I entered the village of Sakuta, which was less than twenty minutes from Bafodia, my mother's usual final destination, I saw our Land Rover parked and my mother sitting on the veranda of one of her customers. As soon as she saw me, there was a big smile on her face and then she started to laugh. Believe me, she could not stop laughing. She said to me "What are you going to do? Take me on that motorcycle?" I said "yes." It seemed funny to her, but it was also dangerous. I sat on the motorcycle seat and she sat on the back. At first, I thought it was cool, but slowly, I began to realize how much she had struggled for us and how difficult it was for her to do her business every week and also take care of us. I was almost in tears when I turned around and looked at her there on the back of my motorcycle. When we got to the next village, I asked her if she would like me to go back alone to Kabala, and then come for her with our Toyota truck, which was being fixed at the shop there. She told me to continue but not to speed. On our way back, it rained, which made it dangerous, especially when the roads got very muddy. We both got wet. After we returned, it stopped raining. It took several hours for our clothes to dry, even in the strong wind. We had arrived in Kabala safely in about three hours. When she got down from the motorcycle, she told my father that she never believed that I could control the motorcycle and that she was very nervous, but she never wanted to let me see it for fear that I would panic. This lady was tough and hard working! Unfortunately, the Land Rover had a major engine problem that needed to be repaired. Since we could not find the parts in Kabala, my mother sent the driver to another town, called Makeni, to buy the parts and return within a day to get the vehicle fixed. The driver left his helper to stay with the Land Rover so no one could take anything from it. It took approximately two days to fix the Land Rover and then it was ready for its next Sunday trip.

Chapter 3

Our Daily Routines

Almost every morning my father would wake me up around 5:30 am to help him make his Lebanese coffee. He took his coffee very strong without any sugar. It was very similar in taste to cappuccino. Once he got up, he would perform his morning prayers and then drink his coffee before taking his morning walk. While his was drinking his coffee, I would do my homework or read one of my literature books assigned by my teacher. I read books like *Robinson Crusoe, Treasure Island, Swiss Family Robinson, Rapunzel,* and other classics. I especially liked reading while I enjoyed the aroma of my father's coffee. After he finished his coffee, he would go out to walk for about an hour. He walked very slowly through the town with some of his friends. Around 7:00 am, before I left for school, he and I would open our store. He would sit and just wait for my mother to wake up and join him. Once my mother got to the store, they would engage in conversation for about an hour until it was time for his morning nap. You see, my father was approximately eighty years old when I was in tenth grade. Being the last child, I was very close to my father. He gave me excellent counsel when it came to religious, educational, and social matters. I was never left wondering about the answer to all my religious questions. I would sit next to him whenever he engaged in religious discussions with some of the religious people in town. In fact, some of them would come to him to answer questions that they had been discussing, while others would come to see him for an interpretation of certain verses or surahs (chapters) from the Holy Quran. He would translate the Holy Quran into Creole, which was the main language spoken in Sierra Leone and by the people who came to visit him. He always used humor to explain difficult concepts or ideas. I really enjoyed listening to him during these times.

Due to his old age, he got tired easily and needed frequent naps, especially in the morning and late afternoon. When he was not napping or talking to my mother, he read books. I tell you, this man loved to read. I strongly believe that I got my love for reading from him. He would read for hours each day and he was well read when it came to Islam and Middle East politics. He had a very strong command of the Arabic language, which is the language of the Holy Quran.

I remember one day when he was reading one of the newspapers he got from Saudi Arabia about Middle East issues, when I saw a fly buzzing around his coffee table. I got a towel, folded it, and took a swing hitting the fly and also the table. My dad was so mad at me when the towel hit the table that he chased me out of the shop. As I started running away, he started to laugh. He got a big kick out of that. He then called me to come back. He looked at me and said, "why did you decide to kill that fly with a towel and bang the table so hard?" I really did not have an answer for that other than that I really wanted to kill the fly. He continued by asking me if I'd known he was taking a nap. I said "yes." Then he said if I were to do it again, he would not hesitate to punish me. I promised him that I would not do it again. He then asked me to tell Pa Kamanda, the cook, to bring us some food so we could have lunch together. I really loved this part of my dad. One minute he was mad at me, and the next we were having lunch together. We really enjoyed the food. It was rice with beef and some vegetables. My father's habit was to eat a small meal four to six times a day, except for dinner, which was the big meal for us. He also took his time when he was eating. He never rushed.

I remember one day when someone stole my father's watch. In fact, it was his favorite watch that he brought with him when he performed his pilgrimage to Mecca, Saudi Arabia. Performing the pilgrimage is one of the five pillars of Islam. It is required of every Muslim to perform this pilgrimage at least once in a lifetime. My father, I believe, went on his pilgrimage around 1966. Upon his return from the pilgrimage, my mother painted our house and decorated it with beautiful decorations in order to surprise him. He enjoyed the changes, but he soon realized that his watch was missing. He then gathered everyone, including his children, and asked them to go to one of the rooms in the house, one at a time, and grab a rope with oil on it that was strung from one end of the room to the other. He directed each person to hold the rope and drag his/her hands along it, and if he or she was the one who stole the watch, then that person's hands will not be released, instead it will stick to the rope. Each one of my brothers went through and almost all the other people who worked for us, except for one of our workers who came out without any oil on his hands. When my father saw that, he asked the man, "Where is my watch?" The worker did not know what to say at first, but he started carrying on and pleading for my father not to call the police about him. In response, my father promised him that if he gave the watch back, my father would forget about everything and let him go free. You see, my father's idea was that the person who stole the watch would not dare to pass his hands along the rope for fear that his hands would get stuck and, therefore, his hands would be dry, and that is what my father was looking for. The person with the dry hands was the one who stole the watch. This was just one of his creativities.

My mother might not eat each meal with us every day. Her favorite time to eat was during dinner. She loved to see everyone sitting at the dinner table and enjoying her cooking or Pa Kamanda's cooking. She cooked the difficult Lebanese foods that Pa Kamanda did not want to cook or did not know how to cook.

In the summer of 1980, my father started complaining about body aches, difficulties breathing at times, and severe headaches. After getting a few shots from the local doctor in Kabala, my father finally decided to go to Freetown, the capital city of Sierra Leone, for further tests and medical treatment. He stayed with a very close relative in Freetown who took him to a doctor. Medication was prescribed for him. For some reason I didn't understand at the time, I was asked by my adopted brother, Farrah, to accompany him to Freetown and to bring our father back to Kabala. My stepbrother and I went to see my father at his cousin's house in Freetown. His cousin, Ali Shaban, who was also the father-in-law of my brother Hanney, was very nice to him. His children treated my father with respect and took care of him while he was sick. When we saw him, he did not look well at all. He was weak and did not have the stamina to walk the way he used to. We contacted our oldest brother, Faiad, who came right away to see my father. We arranged for my father to take the next flight to Kabala since he was too weak to sit in a vehicle for the ten- to twelve-hour trip to Kabala. The flight to Kabala normally took just one hour. We met some friends at the airfield and told them to take care of my father on the flight until he arrived at our home in Kabala. As soon as we said good bye to him, we left for Kabala by road in Farrah's Mazda pick-up truck. We arrived almost twelve hours after my father arrived. My mother told us that she felt he was doing fine and that he was now well. This was a big surprise to us, because when I remembered how he was in Freetown and when I now saw him sitting next to my mother, he looked like two different persons. I finally realized that he never wanted my mother to worry or to be scared, so he pretended that everything was fine with him. He cared for her so much that he did not want to show her that he was really sick. As soon as I realized this, I asked the town doctor to visit us and do some tests. The doctor told me that he had T.B. and that it did not look good at all. The medication that was prescribed to him by the doctor in Freetown was continued, but he never really improved. His health was deteriorating. I started seeing my father getting weaker and weaker each day. He used to awake around 4:00 or 5:00 am and now he wouldn't wake up until 8:00 or 9:00. This was how we knew he was really sick.

One thing I remember that my mother and I did at first was to downplay to each other how sick my father was. I would always try to downplay his condition for fear that something would happen to upset my mother, and I never wanted her to worry too much about my father's health, and she would do the same to me. So, in the end, we both realized that each one of us should just come out honestly and work toward helping him recover. At one point, my brother, Muhammed, took me aside and told me that he, too, was worried about our father's health. We discussed things we needed to do to help him, especially being with him all the time so he would not get lonely.

Chapter 4

The Final Days of My Father

Today was not a good day at all. It was October, 10, 1980, and I was in class at approximately 10:00 am looking through our classroom window when I saw our Land Rover pull up and the driver looking for me. At that time, I was attending Kabala Secondary School, which was a Roman Catholic school run by the Catholic Mission of Sierra Leone. This school was approximately a mile away from our home, and it was a good twenty to twenty-five minute walk. It was one of two secondary schools in Kabala at that time. Although my father was a religious Muslim, he appreciated most of the values of the Catholic religion. He was proud of the fact that my siblings and I were getting the good education offered by the Catholic school. In fact, on many occasions, he would discuss with me the similarities between Islam and Catholicism.

Oh, I thought, this is not good. I knew I had not left my Dad in a healthy condition. In fact, before I left that morning, I kissed him on the forehead and told him I would be back soon. He responded by nodding his head. You see, he had been sick for approximately two months now, and his condition had been deteriorating almost every day. Each day, we heard something new about his health from the local doctors. My brothers Muhammed and Faiad encouraged me to go to school so I would stop worrying about my father's health. It was hard for me to leave him knowing that my father's health was in such a very poor condition. I could not concentrate on anything except his health.

So, when I saw our driver, Amadu, I did not like it at all. When I got out of class, I looked at him and he did not say a word. Oh, I said to myself. I hope he is not going to give me the worst news—that my hero had passed away. My dad was always my hero in every aspect of my life. I opened the car door and did not say a word. I did not even look at Amadu. He started the engine and took off without saying a word to me. I was anticipating the worst. On our way, I was looking for signs of people crying, talking in groups, or doing anything that would suggest that my father had passed away. I finally realized that my mother had sent him to pick me up since my dad's situation was deteriorating rapidly and she needed me by her side and at my father's side.

When we got home, it was not a good scene. My mother was sitting down, which was unusual. Whenever she sat in her chair, it meant she was thinking, confused, or just worrying about something. She was not the kind of lady who just sat around. She had left the bedroom where my father was because she could not handle the situation. He was, as I finally noticed myself and after talking with the doctor, in the last days of his life. When I went to the room where my father was, I saw my older brother, Faiad, sitting on the steps. I did not like this at all. As soon as he saw me, he asked me if I would like some fried plantains. He knew I like fried plantains and that was his way of directing my attention away from my father. When I looked at Faiad more closely, I saw that his eyes were filled with tears. I never answered his question. He called on our cook, Pa Kamanda, to fry some plantains, which he did. I started to enter the room. My brother, Muhammed, was sitting on the floor by my father's side. As soon as he saw me, he stood up and smiled pretending that everything was ok. Oh, no, no, no. It wasn't. I saw my dad just lying in bed, not moving. My hero was not the same anymore. I looked at him again, and he just moved his eyes, his big green, beautiful eyes, from side to side and did not say a word. "What is going on?" I asked my adopted brother, Farrah. "Don't kid me, now!" Farrah was so devastated that he started crying as soon as he saw me. So, here in the room, was our favorite person in the whole wide world lying in bed and unable to do anything.

All four of us sat inside the room just looking at my dad. We did not say a word to one another for about ten minutes. Then, suddenly, I broke the silence by asking my father if he would like to say his noon prayer while in bed. He did not say a word. He just looked at me for a minute then closed his eyes. I then asked him if, after I said my prayer, it was ok for me to say his on his behalf. He opened his eyes and nodded without saying a word. This was the most challenging part for me. Here was the man, the leader, the father, the hero who always led the prayers when we prayed. Here was the man who led prayers at the town mosque. Now, he could not perform his own prayers. He was bedridden and could not even get up. I asked myself many times what would happen if he passed away? I walked out quietly. I went to the washroom and then back to the room where my father was lying in bed.

When I had finished both of our prayers, I could not go immediately to the shop to see my mother. I went to the kitchen to speak with Pa Kamanda, who was preparing dinner. He knew no one was in the mood to eat, but he prepared it anyway. He started talking to me, but his words became choked and tears were coming down his cheeks. Let me put it simply—no one was in a good mood. I finally decided to go to my mother in the shop. This lady was strong, resolute, and assertive but, at the same time, passionate and emotional. When she saw me, she started crying. Many customers came to buy items from the shop, but her mind was on my father's condition. She could not concentrate on the customers. In fact, when a few customers came and they realized that my father's condition was not good at all, they went to the back of our house to see if there was anything that they could do to help. There was not a single person in town who did not know our father. He was famous in all surrounding villages and towns for his leadership, piety, and friendship. He was known as "the Pa" or Alhaji Faiad. The word "pa" is a sign of respect. It is used to refer to older adults and heads of households.

What could I do? At age 17, I was the youngest of all my own siblings but the only ones who were present then were my stepbrothers from my father's previous marriages. My other brothers and sisters from my mother's side were in the U.S. or Nigeria. So, her comfort came mainly from me alone, and it was too much for me to handle. I've always wished my other brothers and sisters had been around to share the burden, especially the emotional roller coaster that I was going through in dealing with the terminal illness of my father, the challenges of my mother and my Aunt Zahideh, and other related problems. My siblings in the U.S.—Hanney, Adbul, Naaman, Samir, and Samira—were unaware of our daily life in Kabala. I believe, to a certain extent, they were also unaware of our father's grave health situation. This was a huge challenge for me and my half brothers. My father, on days when he could talk, would ask about all my brothers and my sister who were in the U.S., and my sister who lived in Nigeria. He always asked about each one of them. He really missed them. We could always hear that in his voice.

My brother, Hanney, was the first one to leave Sierra Leone to further his studies in the U.S. Most of our family members were privately uneasy and asking themselves if this was the beginning of major changes in our family. I was under 10 years old when he left. He was helped by a Peace Corps volunteer named Mr. Broussard, who was teaching, I believe, math or English, at the local secondary school. Mr. Broussard convinced my brother to go to the U.S. and get a better education. I remember a few days before my brother left for the U.S., my father told Mr. Broussard, "You have convinced my son Hanney to go to the U.S. I just want to tell you that it feels like someone is taking a part of me away." I could see my father's eyes were filled with tears. In fact, the day my brother left, both of my parents almost avoided saying goodbye to him. After the vehicle drove away, my mother went to her room and stayed there for almost the entire day, just crying. My father just glued himself to his comfortable chair and read books while he sipped Lebanese coffee. I was sent by my father to check on my nephew, Hussein, who was sick. When I got to my aunt's house, she was crying. When I asked her about Hussein, she could not even say a word. I had never seen my parents and my aunt this sad. Everyone was emotional due to Hanney's departure. This is how the road to the U.S. started.

The second to follow was my brother Naaman, then Samir, then my brother Abdulrahman, and a few years later my sister, Samira. Although it was difficult for my mother, father, Aunt Zahideh, and my step- and adopted brothers, it was not as difficult as Hanney's departure. To a certain extent, I believe they just got used to it. My other brothers were confused since they were the only siblings left in Kabala, beside me and my stepsister, Zainab. My brother, Hanney, paved the way for everyone else to emigrate to the U.S. for a better life. We all benefited a lot from this first step that he took, since we all eventually followed suit after him. Whenever my father would ask about my brothers and complain about how much he missed them, my mom always tried to comfort my father by saying that they were all doing fine. She was happy that they were in the U.S. for a better life, but, unfortunately, it was at the expense of my father's feelings. My mother knew the value of a western education, especially one from the U.S. She worked very hard to send my brothers and my sister to the U.S. to continue their education and become professionals in their respective fields of study. She never settled for sub-standard education. My mother came to love the U.S. and decided to send my brothers to the U.S. after her long relationships with many Peace Corps volunteers. Every time one of the Peace Corps volunteers would visit my mother, he or she would join us for lunch or dinner depending on the time of their visit. They always loved my mother's Lebanese coffee. She would discuss many different issues with them, especially about education in the U.S. and the costs of tuition and other school-related items. One of the Peace Corps volunteers named Susan was very close to my mother. She was a secondary school teacher at a school in Kabala. She taught English and other courses at the school. This lady would visit my mother after school around 5:00 pm and on the weekend. At night, we would wait until she showed up to have dinner with us. My father always teased her about getting married. She would always respond by telling my father that if he found her a husband with the same personality as my father, she would marry him. Then they would both laugh. When it was time for Susan to leave Kabala for the U.S. for good, she could not say goodbye to my mother. I went to visit her at her house to say goodbye. She almost did not open her front door. She told me to not say goodbye because it was too emotional for her. She started crying when I left and I said to her, "May God be with you on your way back to the U.S." She gave me a note to give to my mother. When I went back home, I read the note, too, and my mother looked at me with tears in her eyes and said, "I wish the Peace Corps would extend her stay and send her back to Kabala."

There was another couple named Mike and Nancy who worked for the United Nations Development Program (UNDP). Both husband and wife were also very close to my mother. They would visit her at least twice a week for coffee and lunch. My mother treated all of the U.S. citizens who were working in Kabala on different projects very well. She always admired them for their dedication in helping the people of Kabala.

Based on her interactions with all the Peace Corps volunteers and other Americans who were staying in Kabala, she finally concluded that the U.S. was the best place for my siblings. In the long run, this came to be the best decision she ever made, but with a few disadvantages. One of the biggest disadvantages was the fact that since my mother lived in Sierra Leone and Lebanon and only visited the U.S. and stayed with my siblings for just a few months, they grew apart emotionally, which sometimes made it difficult to relate to her. Sometimes, my siblings did not know how to effectively interact with my mother, which led to minor disputes and hurt feelings. As the Arabic saying goes, El Booed Jaffa, which simply means that distance creates dryness.

My father did not now have the opportunity to be with them or to eat dinner or lunch with them on a daily basis. Our dinner table was empty now compared to the days when everyone was home. When everyone was home and we sat down at the dinner table, we hardly had any space for visitors or friends. My dad would sit on a very comfortable couch and next to him on the same couch would sit my brother, Abdulrahman. Abdulrahman was not the favorite in our house. He did not get along with many of the family. My father was the most tolerant when it came to Abdulrahman. My mother always sat on her own chair next to my father and then my sisters, Samira and Fatima, and brother, Samir, and sometimes my nephew, Munir, and I would all sit around the table for dinner. We would wait for my father to begin eating and then we would all start eating. The food always came with Lebanese salad, which was very delicious. My brother, Naaman, never joined us for dinner since he lived with my aunt. After my brothers, Abdulrahman and Samir, my sister, Samira, and my nephew, Munir, had gone to America, my half brother, Ali, started to join us for dinner every night. However, the dinner table was not the same anymore. It was not full and there were none of the arguments that used to entertain us all. There was no screaming from my mother and no yelling from my father to urge everyone to get along or to eat the food that sometimes my siblings did not like. It was a very quiet dinner table. Now my mother, my father, sometimes my brother Ali, and I would sit at the dinner table and eat our food without much discussion. My brother Ali would always discuss the problems that he was having with his insurance company and how they refused to pay for his vehicle after it had been involved in an accident. My father would always get frustrated at him for not being able to get the insurance company to pay for his car damage.

You see, my brother Ali was a relatively quiet man who liked entertainment and would avoid hard work. He was very friendly, religious, and would always wear a big smile on his face. He married Zahra and they had two boys. Whenever he came to see my father, he would sit down and talk to him for about an hour. The conversation would usually involve many questions from my dad and Ali would do his best to answer them. Ali also had children from his other wives who were also in Kabala. I enjoyed the visits from all of his children. On some days, when they came to visit my father, Ali would give me some money to take them to the market and buy them some toys. We would all play with the toys together. When it was time for them to leave, my father would tell them to come back and visit him again.

One day, when Ali was talking to my dad, well, answering questions, my brother Mohammed came to see how my dad was doing. Muhammed lived just a few minutes away from us. He ran the town's cigarette store and would always make sure my dad got his daily supply of his favorite brand of cigarettes, Lucky Strike. Our half-brother Farrah, who was the owner of the store, made sure that the weekly orders of cigarettes always came with at least one or two cartons of cigarettes for my dad. So, when Muhammed walked in, he greeted my father and everyone. As he was talking, my brother Ali was sneezing. When Ali sneezed, he was really loud. Muhammed pretended to have fallen down due to Ali's sneezing. My dad started screaming at Ali for causing Muhammed to have fallen. It was all a joke. This is how we enjoyed one another. We were just playing. It was really fun when we were all together.

You see, my brother Muhammed lost his voice when he had pneumonia at a very young age. My father, based on what my older brothers told me, took him to different hospitals and did many medical tests to help my brother regain his voice, but they were unsuccessful. Muhammed could talk, but only by whispering. In order to hear him clearly, we had to stand as close as possible to him. In the early sixties, my father sent my brothers Muhammed, Abdulrahman, and Hanney to Lebanon to study Arabic. They attended a school in Tyr, a city in

South Lebanon at a school called Jaafariyeh. They stayed with my grandparents from my mother's side on weekends and holidays. They lived in Lebanon while attending school for almost six years. Then they were brought back to Sierra Leone where Hanney and Abdulrahman continued their schooling, while Muhammed got married. One of the main reasons for bringing them back was financial difficulty. When they came back, my father opened an Arabic tutorial center at our house where all three of them, Adbulrahman, Hanney, and Muhammed, taught the town children Arabic and Islamic studies. Almost all the Lebanese families in the town registered their children at the center.

Our house was always full of activities—interesting and challenging activities. When my half-brothers got married and my other brothers and my sister left Sierra Leone, our house became a little boring. From the Arabic tutoring center and the businesses run by my brothers, to the gathering at our dinner table, there had never been a dull moment at our house. But, after they left, our house became empty.

One of the most difficult and emotional situations at the now-empty dinner table was my father's frequent reading of letters he received from my brothers who were staying in the U.S. Almost every day, someone would go to the post office to get our mail, and the biggest hope each time was to receive letters from my brothers and sisters. Our mailbox number was 14, and I am sure it was one of the mailboxes that received the most mail. In fact, the night guard of the post office was Pa Kamanda, who was also our cook. So, whenever the mail arrived in Kabala, he would tell my mom or dad the next morning when he came to work for us. Usually I was sent to pick up the mail. This was a very exciting task that I really loved to perform. I just loved the smiles my dad and my mom wore on their faces when they saw the letters or any type of mail from my siblings. My dad never had patience with whoever was reading the letters he received. He would get very restless if the person read it too slowly. He wanted it fast. He would ask me or one of my brother Hanney's friends, Bokarie, to read the letters he received from my brothers. He would be sipping his coffee while listening to the reading of the letters with tears coming down his cheeks. I remember one time he received a letter from my brothers, Naaman and Samir. Samir explained in the letter how he got someone to sponsor him to go to school in the U.S. He explained how he was working and at the same time going to school. Naaman explained how he was also struggling with his work and school and how he would love to return and join us because he was not very happy. Also, Naaman explained how, when he arrived in the U.S., my brother Hanney was not home, so he did not know where to go and he was almost arrested for loitering.

My dad's tears were coming down his cheeks just like someone who'd been walking outside on a rainy day. He looked at my mother and said "Why should they be punished and struggling like that?" He continued by saying, "Bring them back, I am here to take care of them." He also mentioned that Naanam had never stayed with him while growing up so he would like to spend some time with him now. In fact, he began making plans about how he would help Naaman open a new business and how they would work together. My mother had never entertained the idea of my brother Naaman or any one of my brothers returning to Africa. But, my dad was so excited thinking that Naaman, and maybe Samir, would be coming back home. Oh, this was such a false hope for him. He told me a story about how he went once to visit Samir in Makeni when Samir was attending high school and was preparing to sit for the GCE, which is a standardized exam for all high school students who have reached form V (12th grade). Anyone who passes the GCE will be accepted to one of the two universities in Sierra Leone. Students who have completed form V are allowed to take it as many times as possible, as long as they pay the fees for the exam. This was what my brother Samir was trying to do. He explained that my brother did not have a bed to sleep on so he bought him a bed and other necessary items, but my dad was not satisfied with the idea that Samir would move to Makeni, which was a town that was approximately four hours of driving from where we lived, to continue his education. He said it was not easy to let my brother move to another town to attend school. Part of his concern was the fact that my brother was only seventeen. To him, my brother was still just a little child.

Every week, my mother would prepare foods, especially Lebanese foods, fruits, and vegetables and send them for my brother, Samir. Almost twice a week, my mother would send me with one of our workers to take a box or two of these packaged foods to one of the pick-up trucks used as a means of transportation to carry passengers from Kabala to Makeni. We would give the driver two to three boxes, and he would ask one of his apprentices to put them on top of the truck. Not only would my mother send food and other items for my brother, she would also send things for the man my brother was staying with, Umaru Jalloh, a family friend and a teacher at the school that my brother attended. When the driver would come back to Kabala from his daily trip to Makeni, my mother would send us to ask him if he delivered the items and if my brother liked them. He would always say yes. I am sure my brother liked every item that he received, especially the delicious bananas and other fruits.

My father did not have the opportunity to discuss daily events or other interesting topics with them. Many times, he would record his voice on a tape recorder and send it to them. This was done in Arabic. He really missed them. In fact, there was an incident when we had to stop the recording of his voice to be sent to my siblings in the U.S. five times due to his getting too emotional and crying. There was not a single day in his life when he did not talk about them, especially how much he missed them. Since I was now the only one of my immediate family at home beside my father, I knew the extent to which he missed them. In fact, on many situations, he had a few heated arguments with my mother, blaming her for pushing his children away from him. It was tough for him. Can you imagine having children living very far away from you? You could not talk with them or even visit them? This was unimaginable and unbearable to him. He once said, "I watched them when they were young, and so the time to enjoy them, to get to know their true personality, to get to know who they are is *now*, but they are gone." This was a missed opportunity for him and for my siblings.

My mother's main goal was for all her children to have a better life, and she believed in education. She believed in the value of a Western education and did not want her children to struggle the way she had. My mother worked very hard to take care of us all, including her stepchildren and my father. She would work long hours at our store and sometimes without a break. She made sure that they all were sent to the U.S. to get an education and to be all that they could be. This was her goal and dream. And almost every one of her children achieved this—but, at the expense of family unity.

After talking with my mother for about ten minutes, I could not handle her crying so I went straight to my aunt Zahideh and asked her to come over. I was very surprised when I realized that my aunt had been avoiding me because she was even more emotional than my mother. She could not even look at me directly in the eye. She started to cry and could not stop. Oh no, I could not handle this. This is too much for me. I am going to have a breakdown. Where is someone who can help? The best way I could handle it was to leave my aunt and go back home. When I got home, my brother Faiad was smoking a cigarette while Farah and Muhammad were in the room with my father. I suggested to them that we go get the town doctor. My mother agreed but asked us to not share with her anything bad that the doctor had to say. Muhammed and I went to get the doctor who was taking his afternoon nap. As soon as he saw us, he said "I know why you are both here." He put on his clothes and came with us. When we arrived, Faiad was almost in tears. He said my father had been moaning and restless. The doctor examined my father and told us to leave the room with the exception of our oldest brother, Faiad. That was a mistake. He thought Faiad was strong emotionally. Faiad started to cry before the doctor even said anything. So, we decided to have him talk to Farrah. Although Farrah handled the bad news that my father had three days at the most, he could not tell it to anyone else without crying. This was tough for all of us. It was not the kind of news anyone wanted to hear, and we did not share this news with our mother. We all gathered in the room where my father was sleeping and just sat on the floor to see if he needed anything or if there was anything that we could do to help him or to ease his pain. Seeing him lying down in bed, with periods of pain, really distressed all of us, especially those of us next to his bedside.

It was Wednesday, October, 13, 1980, when my father's condition deteriorated drastically. The town doctor was called. When he came, he asked everyone to leave the room. My father was given an I-V and I was asked to hold his hands. Almost everyone who knew him personally was at our house. My older brother, Muhammed, came in and looked at me with tears in his eyes. He said to me, "If our father passes away, I do not want you to scream. Instead, I want you to be strong." I thought to myself, well, I will do my best. At approximately 4:15 pm, the doctor came in and told us that my father had just passed away. Muhammed was the first one to start crying and screaming. My mother fainted, and the local nurse had to revive her. I kept staring at my lifeless hero who, a few months ago, was joking with me and explaining about the five pillars of Islam. Each time I looked at him, I never wanted to accept the fact that he had peacefully passed away. I tried to convince myself that he was just sleeping. In fact, I said to myself, "This is not true. He is still alive." I wished this was true. His beautiful green eyes were now closed forever.

While he was still lying in bed, all the brothers came to say prayers for my dad. Farrah could not stop crying. Muhammed was the one who'd been pretending that he was strong, but he kept crying. Once the news reached the local leaders, the town chief instructed his men to beat the drums to spread the news all around the town and to the neighboring towns and villages. The whole town was affected emotionally by his death. People came from all walks of life to pay their respects to him and to comfort us, especially my mother. Below is a poem I wrote when my father passed away.

> Now you decided to leave me during my teenage years.
> Why are you in a hurry to leave me like this?
> You taught me everything that I know.
> You taught me about Islam and how to stay in the right path of Allah.
> I see that your eyes are closed, but I never accepted your passing away.
> I know you are my hero and you never wanted to leave me like this.
> I feel safe next to you and I know you always stayed by my side.
> I am going to miss you. I am going to miss you.
> Oh, no, why did you go and why did you leave me like this?
> I know you once told me that life does not end, but continues in heaven.
> You are now in heaven.
> Good bye, my friend, my father, my hero.
> Good bye, and may Allah be with you.

My brothers Farrah and Muhammed sent someone to tell my brothers Faiad and Ali who were in Freetown. You see, Faiad had been with us at my father's side, but the morning before my father passed away, my mother told him to return to Freetown so he could go back to work since he had taken almost a month off from work to be by my father's side. Now we wished he hadn't gone. My mom's decision was based on the fact that father became too emotional when he was around, which was bad in his condition. She had just wanted him to take a few days off. My brother, Ali, was in Freetown and he was the only one who could not come to see my dad before his death. When the news finally reached Faiad and Ali, they came right away to comfort us and to make sure my dad got the proper and best burial. Our assistant driver did not let either one of them drive. In fact, when they arrived at Kabala, Faiad did not even wait for the Toyota truck to stop before he opened the door. He jumped out and ran straight to the room where my dad was lying in peace. Muhammed and Farrah had to restrain both Faiad and Ali from touching my dad and screaming. That was a scene that I shall never forget. When Faiad came out of the room where my father was lying, he took my mother's hand and walked with her outside to the back yard of our house. He said to my mom, "I know I am the oldest son and everyone expects me to lead everything and make all the decisions." My mother responded by saying, "You are his first son, and you *are* old enough to make decisions, and I am behind you." This conversation went back and forth until my mother gave in and said, "Ok, I will make all the decisions." This clearly showed family unity and how working together will bring a family closer. Although my brother Faiad was from my father's first wife, he respected my mom and he showed her he was very comfortable with her being the head of the family after the death of my father.

Well, it had previously been decided that my father would be buried in our backyard. Official permission was granted, and the burial site, which had been chosen by my father before his death, was identified. I remember, when he was sick, he took Farrah and me to our backyard and showed us where he would like to be buried when he died. I still have this vivid memory of him using his right foot to show us where he would like his grave to be. So, after the permission was verified to bury him in our backyard, Farrah and I told the people who were responsible to prepare it. Since my mother's financial situation was not strong, she was a little skeptical about how much the whole process would cost. But, wait a minute! My father had 800 British pounds in our house safe that he had received from my sister. I remember my sister, Fatima, used to send him money in envelopes almost every two months. He would use some of the money to buy what he wanted but saved the majority. This, then, was the money that was used to pay for his grave and other expenses that were incurred. Both my mother and brother, Faiad, were reluctant to use this money for his burial, but I knew they did not have any other choice. They had to use it. This is something I would like my sister Fatima to know. I am sure she never knew about it.

It was around 1:00 pm, when my father's lifeless body was taken to the town mosque for the funeral prayer. The townspeople refused to put him in a vehicle. To show their love and respect for him, he was hand-carried. Hundreds of people followed the procession and filled the mosque. They were all around the mosque, on the streets next to the mosque, inside the mosque, and on every corner. First, the drums were beaten to let everyone know that it was time for my father's burial ceremony. To pay their last respects to my father, there was a 21-gun salute at the police station. After the noon prayer, the town imam, Alhaji Mumammed Sillah, performed the prayers called "salat al jinazzah." I joined in the prayers with my brothers, Faiad, Ali, Mumammed, Farrah, my sister, Zainab, and my nieces and nephews. We could not stop crying while the imam was reading. After the prayers, my father was taken to our house where he was laid to rest. Again, there were more people than our backyard could handle. After the final prayers, my adopted brother, Farrah, thanked everyone in their various local languages and asked everyone to attend my father's seventh- and fortieth-day ceremonies in the days to come. These two ceremonies were packed with people from all over the town and surrounding villages. During both ceremonies, I gave a short speech. During the first ceremony, it got too emotional for me. I remember choking many times and, at one point, I just broke down in tears. My speech during the first ceremony focused on what I recollected from the stories he had told me and things we had talked about. The main point of the speech centered on the idea of dying. My father always explained to me that he never feared dying or facing God, but he was very concerned about how he would die. He never wanted to be sick, especially with a terminal disease. He would quote from the Holy Quran and some of the Hadiths of the Prophet Momammed about life and death. At the conclusion of my speech, I summarized the things he loved doing the most and how he cared for his children, neighbors, and the community as a whole. I remember the first time he saw a doctor in Freetown, the capital of Sierra Leone, he asked the doctor many times if he had cancer. Despite the many times the doctor said no, he always feared the disease. But, overall, both ceremonies went very well.

Chapter 5

Life Without My Father

After my father passed away, things changed drastically. My mother and I now lived alone in our very big house and did not have any reason to sit at the dinner table to eat as we used to when my father was alive. In fact, we would just eat at our shop, and, at night, maybe we would sit together for a few more minutes and then just grab something to eat. Dinner was not the same anymore. I started working as an elementary school teacher, which was really fun. I applied at The District Education Committee to teach at a primary school (same as elementary and middle school in the U.S.). English was the language used in school. I was accepted and taught civics and geography. This was challenging since I knew almost all the pupils from our town. It took a while for some of the students to accept me as a teacher, not just a friend or a neighbor. I taught pupils in both class 6 and 7 (sixth and seventh grades). The school was less than a ten-minute walk from my house. My mother would always pick up my salary from the local bank on my behalf. She really did not want me to go away so she was happy with my job at the local school. On many occasions, when I got gifts from the parents of my pupils, she would tell me that she was proud of what I was doing and that she really liked the idea that the parents appreciated me.

My brother, Faiad, who was rarely seen during the days of my father, now frequented our home and always made sure my mother's store was filled with enough merchandise. He would always comfort my mother and get her whatever she needed. Faiad was also the husband of my aunt, but they had been separated for almost ten years. My mother had tried to reconcile their marriage, but to no avail. She had wanted my aunt and her husband, Faiad, to get back together and be a couple again. He went back to Freetown where he was staying when my father was alive until my aunt had to go bring him back when he got really sick. He stayed with us for almost a month and passed away at the age of forty-four. Nobody believed it when he got sick and passed away. He was a quiet, dependable, and independent man who owned his own transportation business. He had traveled to almost every city, town, and village in Sierra Leone. On a few occasions, he even went to neighboring Liberia on business trips. He had many children who came to live with us after his death. So, not only was it shocking for us to hear about his death, but it left a heavy financial burden on my aunt who was also struggling to make sure her children lived a comfortable life.

The other challenging issue we all had to deal with was the sudden death of my brother, Ali. You see, we were all caring for Faiad when all of a sudden, around 3:00 am, we heard a car horn beeping nonstop. When I heard the sound of the horn, my sister-in-law, Zahra, who was Ali's wife, and I were in the bathroom helping my brother, Faiad. Zahra rushed out of the room and ran outside crying. I am sure she knew something that I did not know. After I took Faiad back to his bed, I ran outside and was met by my brothers, Muhammed and Farrah. I really do not even want to recount the memory. It was devastating. Here was my brother Ali who had always been well and very energetic, now dead. My mother couldn't stop crying. Farrah took my mother away to his house and told her to just stay there for a few hours. He came back to our house and told everyone to take it easy and keep everything under control. Muhammed was very careful not to let Faiad know about the death of Ali. Faiad and Ali were from the same mother and they were very close.

With all the crying and screaming, Faiad kept asking what was going on and why people were crying. Almost everyone replied with the same answer, "It's nothing, really." Almost three days later, Faiad passed away. His diagnosis was never conclusive. No one really knew what he died of. All I knew was that he was very sick, became very skinny, and was not even able to walk. To the best of my knowledge, I thought he had cancer, but I might be wrong. He died in a very peaceful way, with all his children and his wife next to his bedside, except for Munir, his eldest son, who was in the U.S. I cannot even explain what the family went through, especially my mother and I. Here we were, burying two of my older brothers less than a year after my father passed away.

At some point, I thought my mother needed psychiatric evaluation. She was saying things that made me so emotional and concerned. I decided to sleep next to her for a few months to make sure that she was fine, especially at night. I did not want to leave her alone. I remember waking up at least twice in the middle of the night just checking to see if she was all right. Although she was strong, losing three very close people within a year was devastating. As for my Aunt Zahideh, who was the wife of Faiad, she was a lot stronger than my mother in those days and she took care of her children like a hawk. She protected and cared for them with the help of my mother, her sister. When Faiad passed away, his youngest son, Hussein, was only eight years old.

I do not think my nephews and nieces really knew what they were going through. It was very difficult for them to lose their father at a very young age. But they were lucky to have a strong mother and a very supportive aunt. In fact, my mother and aunt did not differentiate between their children and nieces and nephews. When I was growing up it took me years to realize that my nieces and nephews were not my brothers and sisters. We were raised very close as one big family. When my brothers, sisters, and I needed anything, especially money, we went to our aunt, not my mother, and when my aunt's children need money, they went to my mother, their aunt. It was as if we had two very supportive and caring mothers.

You see, my mother did not have any relatives in Kabala. When her sister Zahideh, my aunt, joined her, they both became closer and closer. They supported each other through rough times. My mother helped my aunt financially and emotionally whenever possible. I remember there was a time when my aunt had five Hino trucks. These were trucks that were used for commercial transportation. In addition to these trucks, my aunt also owned a general merchandise store and she managed a petrol filling station. My nieces and nephews and I would always wait for gifts from the oil company, AGIP. AGIP is the Italian oil company that owned the filling station. Every year around Christmas time, they would have special promotions that came with little gifts like flashlights, key chains, watches, wallets, and other gift items. I really looked forward to visiting my aunt as soon as I heard that the company had sent her these gifts. She was assisted by my brother, Naaman, in running these different businesses. Whenever my aunt encountered financial difficulties, my mom would provide her with the financial support to pay her debts and keep her businesses flowing smoothly. My brother, Naaman, when discussing his life in Africa with people, especially friends and relatives in the U.S., would forget to mention that he ran my aunt's filling station and the store, and how life for us, and especially him, was a lot better than most people there. He would mention a few bad experiences that he'd had and then blanket the whole history of his life in Africa as a negative one. Yes, we had some challenges, but our parents, especially my mother, made sure that we lived a very comfortable life. We had almost everything we needed. Naaman, at the age of sixteen, had a beautiful motorcycle; he had five Hino trucks and their drivers under his leadership and he was the supervisor of all my aunt's employees. Money, I knew, was never an issue. In those days, a person who had fifty leones (the currency of Sierra Leone) was considered well off. Naaman always had more than that in his pocket every day.

While he was still in Sierra Leone, my brother, Hanney, had his own store and used to live a good life. While he was in high school, and later, in college in the U.S, my mother's financial situation was strong. She was considered a rich woman based on the standard of living in Sierra Leone, especially in Kabala. Hanney had a motorcycle, a pick-up truck, and access to my brother Faiad's vehicles. He was well loved by my parents, especially my mother. My mother would do almost anything for him and give him any financial support that he needed. He used to go hunting every evening. This was his favorite hobby. He would pick up some friends in the evening, get all his hunting supplies, fill-up the gas tank of the Toyota pick-up truck (Stout), and then go hunting for birds and deer in neighboring villages. He would drive for thirty to forty-five minutes, hunt for an hour, then head back home with whatever he had killed, including pigeons. He did enjoy a very comfortable life in Sierra Leone.

My brother, Abdul, also came to the U.S. After his death in America, Hanney, who lived nearby in Virginia, was sent to Sierra Leone to inform our mother, aunt, brothers, Farrah and Muhammed, and sister, Zainab, about Abdul's sudden death. Abdul had been killed in his car in Washington, D.C. by a robber. This was one of, if not the, darkest moment in our lives that happened in the U.S. When this happened, I was living in Manassas, Virginia, with Hanney. I believe my brother, Samir, was the first one to be informed about my brother being shot in Washington, D.C. Abdul was in the intensive care unit in Greater Southeast Hospital for a few hours before answering to the call of God. When he passed away, we were all devastated. He was about thirty-two years old.

When I heard about what happened to my brother, I started questioning myself as to why I had come to the U.S. For some reason, I had started to accept some of the stereotypes that some people hold—and *thanks a lot* to the media for such stereotypes!—that the U.S. is a violent place and that people get killed easily and sometimes for no reason. I was so scared about living in the U.S. that I started thinking about going back to Sierra Leone to join my mother or to return to Lebanon and continue my education there. Life in the U.S. was fairly good for me with almost two part-time jobs, living with my brother Hanney, then with my brother Samir, and basically enjoying my new homeland. I had different thoughts going through my mind concerning the safety of my brothers. But at one point, I realized that violence can happen anywhere, irrespective of the county where a person is living. In fact, it was after the death of my brother, Abdulrahman, that I decided to make the most of my opportunity and work hard to achieve the highest degree offered in the field of communications. I made up my mind that I would not settle for just a B.A. or M.A. degree, but I would earn a Ph.D. My mind was set and I made every effort for that ultimate goal to be achieved. A year before I received my Ph.D., I went to Lebanon for a visit and became acquainted with Lina, who later become my wife. In 1995, I received my Ph.D. from Howard University in Washington, D.C.

When Hanney met my mother and the rest of our family in Freetown, Sierra Leone, it was not easy for him to inform them of what happened to my brother, Abdul. My mother was on her way to Lebanon for a visit and she was never the same again. Her mental state was not stable and she got irritated very easily. My mother, who used to be very patient and tolerant, now became exactly the opposite. She would always talk about Abdulrahman and she told us about some of the challenges he faced while growing up. No matter how their relationship was, this was her son and she did her best to send him to Lebanon to learn how to read and write Arabic, and she worked very hard to send him to the U.S. I remember very well that when Abdul was ready to come to the U.S. our mother was not in a strong financial situation to buy his ticket and give him pocket money. She sold things that she had never planned to sell just to get enough money for this ticket and a few hundred dollars to take with him. Yes, there were times when they had not gotten along, but many times parents and teenagers do not see eye to eye. His death really affected my mother mentally and emotionally. As soon as she got the news, she continued her journey to Lebanon, and then to perform her hajj pilgrimage to Mecca, Saudi Arabia. My brother Hanney's visit to Sierra Leone was followed by my brother Samir's visit to us. Samir went to see my sister, Samira, who was not married and was living in Congo Brazzaville. Then he saw my sister, Fatima, who lived in Nigeria, and finally my mother and the rest of the family in Kabala, Sierra Leone. Part of the reason for Samir's trip was to convince both my mother and aunt to move from Kabala to Freetown, the capital city of Sierra Leone, which they finally did. When Samir returned to the U.S., he told us that things were not the same anymore in Kabala. Everything had changed and it was a little challenging, especially financially. His decision to move our mother and aunt to Freetown was a wise decision since they were then more accessible to us. All we had to do to contact them was to make a telephone call to Freetown. This was a huge difference from writing letters that sometimes took six months for replies, since Kabala did not have any telephone service or an efficient mail service. In fact, after my mother moved to Freetown, I kept calling her almost every three days and finally convinced her to come visit us in the U.S. She visited us in 1994 and stayed for approximately six months. She was joined by my aunt three months later. She had been in the U.S. twice and had never really liked it. When I called to try to convince her, it was a challenge for me. Finally, she agreed and she stayed with us for almost six months until my aunt followed her. When she first came, she never rested until she brought Aunt Zahideh, too.

Then they both stayed with us for approximately six months until they decided to go to Lebanon and settle there permanently. This was a wise decision, but very challenging. When they arrived at Deirntar, their hometown, which was almost a two-hour drive from Beirut in South Lebanon, they were welcomed by family members and friends. Once some of their siblings realized that my mother was planning to ask them for the many acres of land that she still owned, they never welcomed her in their homes again and everything changed. Since we did not then have our own legal residence in Lebanon, both my mother and aunt moved from one friend's house to another until I went to visit. My visit was prompted by a call I made to the town where my mother and aunt were then staying. I usually called on Sundays to talk to them. Since the town had only a few lines, I sometimes had to wait for hours to get through. This reminded me of the old Andy Griffith TV show where the town operator, Sarah, had to connect people who wanted to talk to each other. On many occasions, Andy would plead to Sarah to free up the line by asking her to tell one of Aunt Bee's friends to hang up. Sometimes, this was what I had to do since many calls came in on weekends. One day when I got the town's operator, who happened to be related to my mother, she told me how horrible their living condition was. I was told that they had moved to a third house now and this was during the wintertime. Where they were living there was no central heating and it was way too cold for my mother and aunt, who had been used to the hot weather in Africa. So, my wife, Lina, and I decided that I should go to get a first-hand look at my mother and aunt's living condition and make the best decision.

I decided to visit my mother and aunt in December of 1996 during our winter school break. I had three weeks off from school so I figured that would be enough time for me to see them, purchase a nice home, and move them in by the end of December. This was not an easy task as it involved money, time, and patience. Buying a home in Lebanon involved major steps and risks. When my plane landed and I got

My mom waiting for my arrival from the airport in Lebanon.

through customs, it was my aunt who was waiting outside. Tears filled my eyes. She did not look very happy or very healthy. This was not the same aunt that I left in Africa who was strong, healthy, and financially secure. She ran toward me and hugged me for almost three minutes. She called the taxi driver who had brought her to the airport to help me load my luggage into the car. She wanted me to sit with them in the front seat, but I refused because she kept crying just from looking at me. I wanted to be out of sight while talking with her about her stay in Lebanon and how she and my mother were handling the "new" environment after being away for a very long time. While in the car, we carried on our conversation focusing on many different topics until we arrived in Deirntar where my mother was waiting. My aunt would occasionally turn her head to the back where I was sitting and made brief eye contact with me just to make sure that I was listening to what she was saying. Whenever she would look away, I would wipe tears from my eyes. Also, on our way, we picked up my sister-in-law, Nayfe (my wife Lina's sister). As soon as we got closer to where my mother was staying, Nayfe did not want me to go inside the house for fear that I would become too emotional when I saw where she was living. Do not get me wrong. The people with whom my mother was staying were very nice and took good care of her. But that place was not for my mother. She had always lived in a very nice home with all the comfort that she wanted. Here she was staying in a home without any central heating and with no running water. There was one small bedroom that was not suitable for one person, and that was where both my mother and aunt stayed. As soon as the car pulled up, she was in the driveway waiting for

My mother and my aunt in our new home in El-Houche, Lebanon.

me. She rushed to the car and opened the passenger door where I was sitting. I got out and she just kept kissing me for almost two minutes. I couldn't look at her. We went in. This was not a suitable home for her. She deserved much better. After we talked for a few hours, I told her I would like to go downtown and visit some relatives and friends. Before I left I gave each one two hundred dollars.

When I went downtown, I visited my relatives and friends, especially my uncle Ali, my aunt Fiaza, and others. As soon as I got back to my mother-in-law's home, where I was staying, I told Nayfe to find me a realtor so I could buy a nice home for my mother and my aunt. The next day, we visited a nice young man named Ibrahim Murtada. Ibrahim was a builder in the city of Sour in South Lebanon. I decided to move my parents (my mother and aunt) to El-Houche because it was a big city with hospitals, shops, schools, supermarkets, and many other useful places. El-Houche is a suburb of Sour. Ibrahim took us to a new building that was almost finished and showed us the last condo left. This was the biggest condo in the building with three huge bedrooms, one huge living room, one dining room, a long hallway, a very big kitchen with a balcony, a nice garden, and two bathrooms. The condo is right next to the beach in Sour. It is a very beautiful home and at the center of El-Houche. I explained my situation to him, and especially my mother's situation. After I gave him a down payment and signed the contract he gave me the keys.

It was a tough deal for me since the payment of the house was $2000 a month for approximately three years. This was practically impossible. I realized that I had to cut down on my spending and drastically cut down on luxury items so that my mother and Aunt Zahideh could live a very decent and comfortable life.

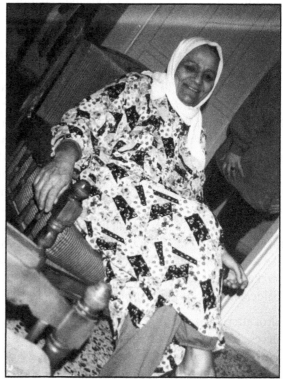

After signing the contract, I did not want to tell my mother and aunt right away. My mother-in-law (my wife Lina's mother) took me to a store owner with whom she had worked out a deal to provide all the appliances. We worked out a monthly payment for all the appliances and he delivered and installed everything. From there, we went to a furniture store, and again, worked out a deal and received the beds, couches, chairs, tables, and all other household furnishings. Now the condo was ready for the move-in. When I visited my mother that very night after I had furnished the home, I

My mother relaxing at her home in Lebanon.

told her that I would return the next day around 10:00 am to pick them up so they could move in. Well, my mother and aunt could not sleep that night. When I came to pick them up, I was told that they already had gone out around 7:00 am and that they were already at their new home. I started to laugh in front of the others, but tears filled my eyes when I returned to see them at the new home. I knew they were overjoyed. As soon I arrived, my aunt met me outside and just wrapped her hands around me and started crying. She said to me "You have brought us our dignity, our prestige, and our lives back. Now we can live like everyone else with all the comfort that we deserve." I just started crying when she said that. My mother was trying to avoid me and she was in tears. She finally came out of the kitchen and said to me "Allah will always be at your side and guide you for what you have done for us." I could not help but cry.

My aunt and mother were two strong ladies who worked very hard in Sierra Leone to raise their families and money had never been a problem for them. Here I was, helping them financially, when, a few years ago, I was just a child going to school and asking both of them for lunch money. My aunt was known for her generosity when it came to both her children and her sister's children. I have to say that it was the best time of my life seeing that I had lifted the standard of living of these two ladies who had rarely suffered financially in their lives. It was a good feeling to know that I was able to lift them up when they were down. I knew back then that my brothers, who had never visited Lebanon, did not understand how things were financially, and did not know what my mother and aunt were going through, trying to adjust to life in Lebanon after almost thirty years of being away from their family. Before I left to return to the U.S., I worked out a monthly allowance that took care of all their utilities, grocery, medical bills, and other related expenses. Also, my siblings, nieces, and nephews would send them money occasionally to help them out. It was nice to see the family come together to take care of them. In fact, those of us who were helping them financially will always laugh about the fact that each one of us was asked to pay for some item that they needed. At first, we would argue and say, "I was the one who paid for such and such." Well, finally, we realized that they would ask each one of us for the same item that they needed. And they ended up getting the money for the item from each one of us. At one point, I asked my aunt why they would ask each of us for money to buy the same item, and she told me, "Well, you are all our children and there was nothing wrong with asking everyone to help out." She concluded her answer by saying, "when we were bringing you all up, no one helped us. We did it on our own. So now is the time to benefit from that." I just laughed and agreed, and then told her that I was hungry and would like to eat some of her kibbah. This is a type of Lebanese food made with ground beef and cracked wheat on the outside, then studded with ground beef, onions, and peppers in the inside. She was famous for making it.

Also, after our mother and aunt settled in EL-Houche and after a few visits by my siblings, nieces, and nephews, almost everyone understood the financial situation of my aunt and my mother and then almost everyone was willing to help out financially, maybe with some occasional grumblings. Many of them would buy household appliances, furniture, and other items

Eating breakfast with my mother and aunt in Lebanon.

that were greatly appreciated. In fact, whenever one of us would visit them, whatever was needed at that time, that person would purchase for them.

Another very positive outcome of buying this home for my mother and aunt was the fact that most of my siblings, nieces, nephews, relatives, and friends could visit Lebanon and my mother and Aunt Zahideh and they would have a place to stay. In fact, within a year of purchasing the home, my brothers, Samir and Hanney, and my sister, Samira, and her family visited my mother and aunt and stayed at the condo. My aunt's children also visited her. I realize now that this had been a very good idea since now anyone from our family, especially siblings, nieces, nephews, and cousins have a place to stay if they visit Lebanon.

At this new place, they made friends and became well known to all the neighbors. The neighborhood children would often come to visit my mother and aunt. These were little children from ages two to ten. They would hang around the house, and sometimes the older ones would do small chores for my mother who would reward them with a few Lebanese pounds or toys that my aunt would get from the toy store. Since we come from a collectivistic culture where people are socially and emotionally connected with one another, all of my family members were very close. In our culture, when our parents retire or cannot support themselves financially, the children are supposed to take care of them. I know this idea of collectivism does not settle well in some cultures, especially Western cultures where the individual is only responsible for himself or herself and just a few close relatives. The support some people provide might not involve financial support since parents are more likely to have a strong retirement. In our culture, our parents' 401K or social security *are* the children. Sometimes, a parent's social security or retirement is based on how many children he or she has and how much financial and emotional support are provided by the children. This is what my mother and aunt enjoyed from all my siblings and cousins. We never wavered in helping them financially and emotionally. I remember that whenever I visited them, it was a daily routine for all the neighbors to visit them just to drink tea, coffee, and sometimes eat lunch or dinner. They attracted people from all ages, social classes, and religious backgrounds. It was always fun meeting all the neighbors and friends on a daily basis. Nevertheless, my aunt's and my mother's focus, time, energy, and most of their money were spent on legally fighting for my mother's land, which consisted of approximately 30 acres in their hometown, Deirntar, and still exists today. They made countless trips to different areas of Lebanon to search for records and deeds and appeared many times in court to gain back their land, but they never succeeded. My mother's daily conversation was centered on the issue of her land and how it was taken away by her family, especially by one of her sisters. This was something that she never forgot, and she never forgave them for it.

Chapter 6

My Mother's Rescue from Lebanon

The summer of 2006 was a very challenging and difficult one for our family, especially for those of us living in the U.S. When the war with Israel broke out in Lebanon, my mother was at her residence in El-Houche, which was the center of the Israeli attacks. It also happened that my older brother, Hanney, was then on vacation in Lebanon visiting our mother. A few weeks before my brother went to Lebanon, I had promised him and my mother that I would join them in Lebanon and stay for at least one month. I made all the arrangements to take my children, and my wife was shopping almost every day to buy the children new summer clothes, toys, gifts for relatives, and other necessary items to take with us. My children were all excited about visiting their grandparents and relatives in Lebanon and spending some time at the beach and with their friends. They always enjoyed making new friends in Lebanon over the summer. Whenever we visit our relatives in Lebanon and it is time to come back to America, my oldest son, Hussein, balks at coming back and wants to stay with his grandparents in Lebanon.

The day I picked up the airline tickets from the travel agency in Washington, D.C., I heard on the radio that Israeli planes were attaching Lebanon, especially South Lebanon, which was where we were going. I thought at first that this would only last a few hours or days. Within twelve hours, the war had spread to other areas of Lebanon, and it escalated with non-stop bombings of some parts of Beirut and South Lebanon. I was very confused and stressed with fear for the safety of my family, especially my mother, my brother, Hanney, my niece, Salha, and others. My wife, Lina, was very concerned for her family, also, since her brothers, who lived in Brazil, were visiting their mother in South Lebanon. The whole situation was upsetting. I had to call the travel agency and get refunds for all tickets I had bought for our trip to Lebanon.

My brother, Hanney, who had never experienced being in a war zone, kept calling us almost every hour asking us if the U.S. was pushing the Israelis for a cease-fire. He was getting very depressed and thought it was just a matter of time before he would be killed. Almost all the surrounding buildings next to my mother's home, where my brother was staying, were under fire with constant Israeli bombings. We were glued to the TV and Internet for daily developments. At one point, I thought we were going to lose our mother, brother, niece, and her children. My siblings and I endured or experienced a roller coaster mentality during the whole ordeal. I constantly waited for a phone call from Lebanon to find out how our mother and the rest of our family were doing, but at the same time, I didn't want to hear the phone ring for fear of hearing bad news. I would call my mother and the rest of my family every few hours to get updates on their conditions and to know whether things were getting better over there. But, as often as I called, I never received the good news I was hoping for. I was always stunned by my mother's calmness and lack of fear about what could happen to her in the war zone. She was, as stated earlier, just a few hundred yards from bombed homes that had been leveled to rubble. All supermarkets, filling stations, stores, bakeries, etc., were closed except for a few of them that would open for less than four hours a day. When asked how she was doing, she would always respond by saying "My life and existence is in Allah's hands." She would also say "What can I do? I am just waiting for a cease-fire to take place one day." In fact, many times she would just tell me that she was drinking Lebanese coffee or eating lunch or dinner. At one point, while watching the news on CNN, I saw a building that was on fire after being bombed by the Israelis. I knew this building was just a few hundred yards from where my mother lived. When I called my mother to ask her how she was doing and if she knew about the bombed building, she just said, "Why are you surprised about the building that was bombed? They are bombing everyone, every building, and everything. It is just a matter of time for our building to be bombed, too." When I heard her, I realized that I had always underestimated my mother's courage and fearless attitudes and to accept the fact that,

Me and my mother at my brother Samir's home in Ashburn, Virginia, U.S.A.

when in a war zone, it is best to stay calm in order to retain one's sanity. Well, my brother, Hanney, was the quite opposite. He was devastated and very worried. Whenever we would call him, he would talk about how he couldn't sleep at night due to the constant bombings, the sound of fighter bombers overheard, and other weapons used during the war. He told me of an incident when he went to a hotel called Rest House Sour that was supposed to be the only safe place. On his way there, the car in front of him was bombed and everyone was killed. He was so devastated that he thought he was going to die any minute. He stayed at the hotel for a few hours and, when the bombings died down for a few hours, he rushed home.

Almost a week into the war, I heard on the radio and on CNN that the U.S. government was evacuating U.S. citizens and permanent status holders from Lebanon. Given the fact that I do not believe everything I hear from both radio and TV, I was constantly on the phone with my mother, brother, and other relatives trying to verify whatever I heard in the news. CNN and the BBC had live coverage of the war. Anderson Cooper's *360 Degrees* program became my nightly edition of news on CNN. I always waited for his show, and then I would call and ask my relatives in Lebanon to make sure what he was saying was in fact true. On many occasions, they could not verify what was covered on CNN. Coming from a strong background in mass communication research and with almost twenty years of teaching mass communication courses, I knew I shouldn't just believe whatever I heard in the news. Agenda setting, which is one of the theories that I teach, discusses how the media prioritize news events every day to gain the largest audience. I found the coverage of the 2006 Israel war on Lebanon to be the most important issue in the news. So, when I heard this news about the plan to evacuate U.S. nationals, I verified the news through different sources. This was great and comforting news, but there was a huge challenge ahead of us. The biggest challenge in getting my mother to the U.S. was to convince her to leave Lebanon. My siblings, especially my brother Samir and I, had to make a tough decision to bring my mother to the U.S. At first, I arranged for my mother to be moved from Sour, where the relentless Israeli bombings were taking place, to Saida, which was relatively peaceful. I had to send some money through Western Union so my niece, Salha, could stay with my mother in a hotel for a few days while she looked for a rental condominium. My brother, Samir, and sister, Samira, added a few hundred dollars to what I had to send for my mother. After a few days at a hotel, she finally found a nice condominium, and my mother and Salha and her children stayed at this rental place for a few weeks. Being able to move my mom and my niece and her children to a hotel in Saida and then to an apartment was a great relief. They were now in a "safe" zone free of Israeli bombings. On the other hand, I was relentless in my emotional appeals to convince my mother to move to the U.S. I finally resorted to asking for the help of Salha to convince my mother to leave on the next available ship that was leaving Lebanon for Turkey, and then leave by air to the U.S.

Arrangements were made for my mother to catch an early bus to Beirut in order to be on the first ship out of Lebanon. Over the phone, we discussed our plan with my niece, Salha, a neighbor, and others who got involved. My mother later told me that on the day that she was supposed to leave Salha and come to the U.S., she got up at approximately 5:00 am, took a shower, drank her morning coffee, some milk, and left her residence to catch the bus. This was all done with the help of Salha. According to Salha, when my mother arrived at the bus stop, she was very emotional about leaving Salha behind. Salha was also very emotional about my mother and her daughter, Samia's, departures. In a few minutes, once everyone was seated in the bus, the driver drove off for the port in Beirut. Once they arrived at the port in Beirut, papers were checked and the embarking started. My mother, based on my conversation with her, was confused and a little disoriented. She had never experienced war or rescue before. The scene was chaotic and hectic. She kept asking me, "Where are they taking me? When will you be at the airport? How long is it going to take?" These were all questions that I answered with just one answer, "Do not worry. Your sons and daughter are waiting for you. Once you get to the U.S., you will be in good hands." After the chartered ship left Beirut, it took almost two days to reach its final destination in Turkey. Once everyone arrived in Turkey, the U.S. military transported all passengers to the Insurlik Airbase in Turkey. At the airbase, medical attention was given to all those in need, including my mother, who was diabetic and needed blood sugar testing and medication.

Based on my daily conversations with Samia, Salha's daughter, and some of the U.S. staff at the airbase, there was plenty of food for everyone to eat during breakfast, lunch, and dinner. At the airbase, there was medical staff, including doctors, nurses, and other medical staff. Also, there were embassy and state department staff to render aid to those who had problems with their passport, permanent residence status, or other documents. When I would call to speak with my mother, the main question was, "When am I going to see you all in the U.S.?" The high number of people who were rescued made it challenging for the U.S. to bring them all home

A family picture of me, my wife, and three of my children.

in a short time. It did take a long time, almost ten days, to transport to the U.S. everyone who left Lebanon at the same time as my mother.

One evening, when I called to speak with my mother, I was told that she was on a bus to the airport to board a chartered flight to the U.S. In a few minutes after I hung up, I received a call from my mother. She told me that I should meet her at the airport upon her arrival. I then called the 1-800 number of the State Department handling my mother's case and got more specific information from the person who answered the phone. We were told that the flight from Turkey would land in Atlanta, Georgia, and then passengers should buy their own tickets to their final destinations. As soon as I got this information, I called my brother, Samir, who worked diligently with his wife, Karen, to purchase my mother and Samia two tickets from Atlanta to Washington Dulles Airport. Once we got the news from the Red Cross volunteer who was taking care of my mother after she arrived at Atlanta, Georgia, we headed for the airport. This was the biggest and happiest news that we all received. I would say that almost everyone in our family was at Dulles International Airport in Herndon, Virginia, waiting for my mother's arrival. While we were waiting for her arrival, we discussed how to take care of her and what we all needed to do to make her stay as peaceful and easy as possible. After waiting for about an hour, we saw her being pushed in a wheelchair by one of the airport's employees. We all rushed toward her and started kissing her. When I got closer to her, I could not look her in the eyes. I knew she had been through a lot. I kissed her on her head and she looked at me and said, "I am really tired and I would just like to rest." We then told her to go with my sister, Samira, and stay with her for a few days. It took a while for everyone to kiss her and

A family picture with my mother.

say hello. Then we all left the airport. When I returned to school the next day, one of my co-workers, Helen Friedkin, noticed how happy I was and she said, "I am sure your mother is now in the U.S." I explained to her how she came and that she is now staying with my sister in Woodbridge.

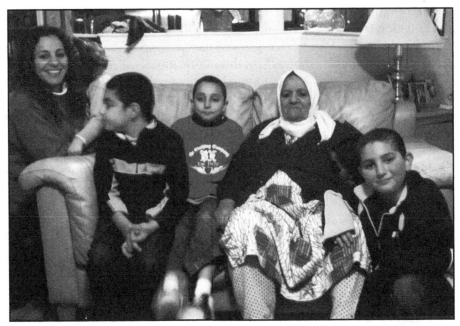

My mother with my family.

My youngest son.

Chapter 7

I Made My Choice to Come to America

My own decision to go to the U.S. and further my education was a very complex and challenging one. In fact, toward the end, it wasn't mine alone, but a consensus decision by all my siblings and my mother. Before leaving for the U.S., I went to see my sister, Fatima, in Nigeria for a few months in the northern city of Kano. I really enjoyed my stay with her and her family. Her husband, Hussein, is a very kind and intelligent man. As soon as I visited with Fatima, she told me to go to visit family members in Lebanon before going to the U.S. Her goal was for me to get a strong command of my parents' main language, Arabic, to get a first-hand experience of our Lebanese culture, to appreciate what the culture had to offer, and to meet with my parent's relatives. When I visited Lebanon, I stayed for about a year. I got to see all my relatives and spent time with them in different parts of the country. I really loved my mother's hometown, Deirntar, and my father's hometown, Harris. These are two towns next to each other that are approximately fifteen minutes apart by car. It was all really nice and beneficial. Although the civil war was going on, I enjoyed my stay and really gained a lot from it. After a year, I then left for Sierra Leone to join my mother for a few months, and later she finally decided to go visit my sister in Nigeria and then my siblings in the U.S.

After securing my visa for the U.S., I finally went to the U.S. to further my studies. I was very happy to see my siblings. We had not seen one another for almost ten years. I was especially happy to see my brothers Naaman and Abdulrahman. Naaman used to tell jokes, especially when we were around Abdulrahman; Naaman used to tease him a lot. I was also happy to see my mother who was so happy among her children. Although she achieved her goal of seeing almost all her children in the U.S. working and going to school like most people, she never really liked it in the U.S. She always wanted to go back to Sierra Leone. So, a few months after I had entered and settled in the U.S., she decided to go back to Africa.

My first goal in the U.S. was to attend school. I applied and started school at Northern Virginia Community College in Alexandria, Virginia. I took almost sixty credits that were considered general education requirements. After two years at the college, I applied and got accepted to the George Mason University where I received a BA and an MA in communication. I became a graduate teaching assistant in the Department of Communication while I was doing my master's in communication. As a teaching assistant, I worked very closely with professors Don Boileau, Anita Taylor, and Raymond Akwule. That experience paved the way for my career to become a professor of communication. After receiving my MA, I then went on for my Ph.D. in communication at Howard University in Washington, D.C. I secured a scholarship and a graduate teaching assistant position at Howard teaching debate and argumentation courses. While I was at Howard, I was also an adjunct instructor of communication at Montgomery College, Rockville, Maryland, where I finally became a full professor of communication after receiving my Ph.D. at Howard.

Contrary to what I was told about the U.S., life was not easy, especially when going to school and working full-time. When I was attending Northern Virginia Community College, I was also an employee at a local fast-food mart. This was tough for me since I worked from 3–11:00 pm and went to school from 8:00 am until 2:00 pm with a few hours of break between some of my classes. Every night, when I got off work, all I did was take a bath and go to sleep.

At my graduation ceremony in 1995, Howard University.

I did my best to study on weekends and on early mornings. Although it was tough for me to wake up earlier than 7:00 am, I made it a point to wake up around 5:00 am to study for exams, write papers, and do my homework. I found that working on my schoolwork very early in the morning led to good grades and a high quality of work. Once I got started, I always made sure that I finished my school work before leaving the house for school, work, or any other activity. Some mornings, it was so difficult for me to wake up, especially after a very difficult night at work. However, I knew that without a Ph.D., I wouldn't be satisfied. You see, coming from a different culture could create many barriers for me to secure a high-paying job and to receive respect or to reduce any types of discrimination that I might encounter. Education, I believed, was my key to eliminate all of the above, or if not, at least reduce those and other barriers that I might encounter. The U.S., as people say, is a land of opportunity, but you need to work for it. Opportunity does not come looking for you. You have to seek it. And that is exactly what I did.

Although I encountered many stereotypic assumptions, especially after the 9/11 World Trade Center attack in New York City and at the Pentagon, I knew I had to be patient and prove that I was a law-abiding citizen who always strives for a better life for himself and his family. Different cultures have different types of stereotypes, prejudice, and discrimination against other races, religions, and ethnicities. Almost everyone has faced some type of discrimination or prejudice. I remember a situation where a female friend introduced me to her mother. I was really looking forward to meeting her mother. As soon as she saw me, she said "so when are you going to blow up a building and kill people?" Honestly, I did not know what to say for a few seconds. I looked at her and said, "Madam, I teach students and do not blow up buildings. I am a college professor who is an American Muslim. I am proud of being an American Muslim." I further went on to tell her that in every culture, race, religion, or ethnicity, there are bad people. And the bad people in the Muslim faith do not even make up five percent of the population. I told her how my brother, Abdulrahman, was killed while touring Washington, D.C and that I do not find all Americans guilty because of that. After knowing me for a few months, her perceptions started to change. In fact, we discussed the similarities among the three major religions of the world: Christianity, Judaism, and Islam. My goal, whenever I experience a problem, especially a stereotype, is to work hard to prove it wrong. I love meeting people from different cultures and learning about their beliefs, values, attitudes, and behaviors. One of the key ways that I learned a lot about the American culture was just to interact with Americans, especially people from different age groups. These daily interactions provided me with valuable information about the culture and the people. Also, given the fact that the U.S. is a multicultural nation, I never have to go far to find people from other cultures—I get many wonderful students from various cultures.

My acculturation process in the U.S. was challenging, rewarding, and sometimes frustrating. There are some who believe that the culture in the U.S. is like a melting pot, while others believe that it like a salad bowl. Based on my experience, I believe it is like a salad bowl with all the wonderful cultures mixed together to create the wonderful American culture that we all experience and are a part of every day. I really love the American holidays, including,

Thanksgiving, Fourth of July, Halloween, other religious holidays, Memorial Day, Labor Day, and a few others. In fact, my favorite is Thanksgiving where all family members and sometimes very close friends get together for a wonderful meal. In fact, one of the first holidays I learned about and even wrote a college paper on is the history of Thanksgiving. I know sometimes I hear people who say that they do not celebrate Thanksgiving. Thanksgiving is an American holiday that deals with giving thanks for what we have, especially for those of us who can put food on the dinner table. This is not a spiritual or religious holiday, at least to me. In a large family like mine, we do not all see each other every week or every month. Thanksgiving is a chance to meet together, eat, and catch up on family news. I do not allow any stereotype or prejudice to act as a barrier when interacting with people from different cultures in the U.S., especially those from the mainstream American culture. It is through my daily interactions in the U.S. with people from all over the world that I keep increasing my horizons about cultures.

One of the major advantages of going to America is that all of my siblings now live close to me in nearby Virginia, except for my sister, Fatima, who lives in Lebanon. It is very easy to visit each one of them, especially on weekends when almost everybody has time off. When things are going smoothly and everyone is on speaking terms, we normally gather at one of my sibling's houses for dinner. When we do, it is really a time for fun, especially telling jokes and laughing while enjoying our meal.

I consider our family to be living a very comfortable life. Each one is doing well financially and emotionally. My brother, Hanney, who is a professor of computer science at Northern Virginia Community College, is a well-respected professor in the field of computer science. I consider him one of the most friendly and most caring persons that I know. When it comes to interacting with people from different cultures, he always creates bridges, not walls. He does not see the skin color of people or their economic or social status. He accepts everyone as equal. He is close to his children whom he enjoys very much. Although we may not see each other for a few weeks or even months, he is the only one I feel very close to when it comes to going to places, eating out, talking about different topics, or sometimes, just spending time together.

When we get together, it always feels good to know that each one of us has achieved our individual goals, including financial and family goals. Compared to when each one of us first came to the U.S., there is now a huge difference in our standard of living and overall satisfaction. We all had very low-paying jobs while going to school, but after graduating from college and securing professional jobs, life is now much better. If success can be measured by a college degree, living in a nice home, having a professional job, and having a wonderful family with very beautiful children, then my brothers, sister, and I have achieved our American dream and are very successful. Although we had no parents or guardians in the U.S., we never strayed away from the path of a good education and being good citizens. I am very proud of my siblings, especially after what we have achieved. I have heard stories of many immigrants who come to the U.S and, instead of achieving a good education, resort to taking illegal drugs, becoming alcoholics, and going in and out of prison for different crimes. We are quite the opposite. Despite not having relatives or parents in the U.S., or at least someone to guide us, we never resorted to anything destructive or illegal. Instead, we made sure that we attended school and landed professional jobs. This, I believe, is the success story for all my siblings. Yes, we do have our moments when we argue, gossip about one another, and sometimes get very angry at one another, but we have always respected and cared for one another. Deep inside our hearts, we know when we need one another we will stand up and help.

As for my brother Samir, he is a very honest and straightforward person who is not, however, a diplomatic person. Sometimes, he comes across as being harsh and aggressive, which is really not his true personality. I remember in 1986 when he introduced Karen, his current wife, to me, I knew it was going to be a difficult process to get Karen to understand that he is a very passionate person who acts tough but has a big, soft heart. In fact, at his wedding, we were joking around about how long it would take my brother to blow up when he dislikes something and scare Karen away from him. Well, Karen is a nice woman who understood that my brother is a very compassionate person with a soft heart. He reminds me a lot of our father. Our father was very direct, especially when he did not like something. Samir is a biochemist and works as a manufacturing manager for the NCI at the NIH in Maryland. One of my brother's favorite hobbies is to coach kids in soccer. In fact, he does this together with his wife. They are both involved with soccer and two of his children are now playing sports in college.

My brother, Naaman, is a very interesting person. He loves his siblings but does not always show it. He loves to have everyone gather at his house for lunch or dinner and tell jokes while eating. He loves to tease friends and relatives—this is his way of entertaining guests. I find him to be a very hard-working person who always would beat the odds when he faced difficulties. He went through two bitter divorces and came out of those as a strong person who always strives for a better life. When he stayed with me in 2000, before he got married to his third wife, he frequented the area mosque, fasted during the month of Ramadan, and practiced a few aspects of the Islamic religion. I loved that part of him when he got closer to Allah. I know deep inside his heart, he is a kind person but sometimes, through his choice of words or language, he comes across as having strong opinions about people or events. He is the kind of person who would enjoy discussing different topics with anyone who is around. Based on my daily conversations with him and my brother, Samir, is it evident that he is very happy with his third wife and with his beautiful children from his previous marriages and his current marriage.

When my sister, Samira, joined us in 1997 with her husband and family, we were very excited. Samira had lived in the U.S. from 1978–1984 and then she left from 1984 until 1997. When she got married in 1984, she left for Congo Brazzaville until the war broke out there in 1997. She then went to Lebanon and stayed with my mother for a few months and then came to the U.S. to finally settle down. She came with five children who attended middle and high school here in the U.S. while she ran her dollar store in Woodbridge, Virginia. It was nice to have our sister join us since we were all boys. She went through some difficult times from helping her children and husband with the English language, to opening a store and adjusting to the "new" way of life. A few years ago, two of her daughters got married and now each has a son.

Looking back at all the worries, challenges, sufferings, achievements, and successes, I have to say that in the end, things did not fall apart. Each day I stand in front of my students in a classroom, I just want to impart as much knowledge to them as possible. I try to teach them that life is what you make of it. Although there are challenges out there, a person's measurement of achievement is determined by how the difficulties or challenges are handled and how much patience is practiced. I remember when my mother came to stay with us for a while during the 2006 Israeli bombardment of Lebanon—she had almost five homes at which she could stay. Each one of her children, including myself, had a beautiful home. In fact, during her short stay in the U.S., she stayed in each home for a week or so.

Although there were some internal challenges and misunderstandings among us, we were relentless in our effort to help her adjust to life in the U.S. At one point, when it was my turn for her to stay with me, I sat with her on my deck just looking back and discussing our past and how she struggled to take care of everyone, including my father. We were joined by my closest friend, Eric, who would visit my mother almost every day when she was with me. She looked at me and said, "Finally, it feels so good to see all of you, my children, living to their highest potentials. My dream was to get everyone to the U.S. and to become productive citizens with at least a college education." She further explained to me that it was hard to hear my father's constant complaints of her decision to send everyone to the U.S. She explained to me how sometimes, when she missed all of my siblings so much, she would go to bed in tears, but would hold back crying in front of my father. She agreed that it was difficult to send everyone to the U.S. and leave my father without most of their children, but she knew there was not a better future for them in Kabala. She concluded by saying, "I wish he had lived until today to see all of you, to visit all of you, and to see how the family has grown and become very successful." She got a little emotional when she said, "I cannot thank Allah enough for all the success of my children in the U.S."

My friend, Eric, who was visiting us again, understood very little of what my mother said, but he understood that my mother was happy and satisfied with her children's success. She admitted that once in a while she knew there were disagreements and sometimes heated arguments among her children, but that when one of us is in need of help, we would all join hands and offer assistance. "Yes, you all argue, you all sometimes talk behind each other's back. Yes, you all sometimes cannot not stand one another, but I know, and I have witnessed it, that if one of you is in trouble, is sick, or needed help, you will all come together and join hands to help out" she said. Based on our conversation, I knew that she knew that some of our family members, not necessarily my siblings, sometimes exaggerate our personal problems with each other. To that end, she told me not to listen to what others say about my siblings, but to interact with them directly. At the end of that particular conversation, I concluded that things, in the end, did not fall apart. My mother came to the U.S. to see her dream for her children come true and she was completely satisfied with her original decision to send them to the U.S. I looked directly into her eyes and said, "We knew what your ultimate goal was, and we did our best to achieve it."

After my aunt passed away in 2005 from internal bleeding following heart surgery, my mother gradually became restless, confused at times, and difficult to deal with. When she visited us in the U.S. during the 2006 Israeli war in Lebanon, she stayed for just a few months and then went back to Lebanon where she passed away peacefully in 2007, almost two years after the death of my aunt.

Conclusion

Members of my family are deeply emotional, and they have a strong sense of mission. As a young man my father moved from his native Lebanon to Sierra Leone where he raised a large family and instilled in them and in his community the values of Islam and a sense of morality. He now lies in our backyard in Kabala, Sierra Leone under the shade of one of his favorite trees. He accomplished his mission.

My mother chose to spend her last years in her native Lebanon, but not before she had the satisfaction of reminding her grown children in America of the lessons she had first taught us when we were growing up in Sierra Leone. She chastised us anew for our shortcomings and praised us for our accomplishments and our love for one another. We all benefited from our second chance to hear her wisdom.

As the head of a beautiful growing family and a teacher of young adults at university and community college, I find great satisfaction in my opportunities to learn and grow as a human being and to give confidence to others. The everyday decisions we make, as well as the major decisions of our life, all draw upon the observations and experiences of our earlier years. Doubt and disappointment are a part of life. but don't be discouraged. If we remain true to our vision of leading a good life, we become more resourceful and inspired and we find our way.

List of Family and Friends

Hajj Abu Faiad	My father
Haja Oum Hanney	My mother
Lina	My wife
Farrah	Adopted brother
Faiad	Stepbrother
Ali	Stepbrother
Muhammed	Stepbrother
Zainab	Stepsister
Hanney	Brother
Abdul	Brother

List of Family and Friends

Fatima	Sister
Naaman	Brother
Samir	Brother
Samira	Sister
Munir	Nephew
Amadu	Driver
Salha	Niece
Samia	Salha's daughter
Zahideh (Oum Munir)	My aunt
Faiza (Oum Abdallah)	My aunt
Nayfe	My wife Lina's sister
Hajj Ali (Abu Hussein)	My uncle
Sieh	House helper
Pa Kamanda	Our cook

Notes

Notes

Notes

Notes